HEALTHY HABITS

WASHING UP

by Emma Carlson Berne

Consultant: Beth Gambro
Reading Specialist, Yorkville, Illinois

BEARPORT
PUBLISHING

Minneapolis, Minnesota

Teaching Tips

Before Reading

- Look at the cover of the book. Discuss the picture and the title.
- Ask readers to brainstorm a list of what they already know about washing up. What can they expect to see in the book?
- Go on a picture walk, looking through the pictures to discuss vocabulary and make predictions about the text.

During Reading

- Read for purpose. Encourage readers to think about washing habits as they are reading.
- Ask readers to look for the details of the book. What are they learning about how to wash to stay healthy?
- If readers encounter an unknown word, ask them to look at the sounds in the word. Then, ask them to look at the rest of the page. Are there any clues to help them understand?

After Reading

- Encourage readers to pick a buddy and reread the book together.
- Ask readers to name two reasons to make washing up a habit. Find the pages that tell about these things.
- Ask readers to write or draw something they learned about washing up.

Credits:
Cover and title page, © Ecaterina Glazcova/Shutterstock, © Artazum/Shutterstock; 3, © ksena32/Adobe Stock; 5, © Artazum/Shutterstock, © Userba011d64_201/iStock; 6–7, © Artazum/Shutterstock, © PeopleImages/iStock; 8–9, © nateejindakum/Adobe Stock; 11, © nobeastsofierce/Adobe Stock; 12–13, © PeopleImages/iStock; 15, © Image Source/iStock; 16–17, © Kostikova Natalia/Shutterstock; 18–19, © xfgiro/iStock; 21, © MelkiNimages/iStock; 22T, © HughStonelan/iStock; 22M, © Africa Studio/Adobe Stock; 22B, © Natasha Zakharova/Adobe Stock; 23TL, © BM_27/Shutterstock; 23TM, © Paulista/Adobe Stock; 23TR, © MOZCO Mateusz Szymanski; 23BL, © Elizaveta Galitckaia/Shutterstock; 23BM, © showcake/Adobe Stock; 23BR, © Lana Langlois/Shutterstock.

STATEMENT ON USAGE OF GENERATIVE ARTIFICIAL INTELLIGENCE
Bearport Publishing remains committed to publishing high-quality nonfiction books. Therefore, we restrict the use of generative AI to ensure accuracy of all text and visual components pertaining to a book's subject. See BearportPublishing.com for details.

Library of Congress Cataloging-in-Publication Data

Names: Berne, Emma Carlson, 1979- author.
Title: Washing up / Emma Carlson Berne ; consultant, Beth Gambro, Reading
    Specialist, Yorkville, Illinois.
Description: Minneapolis, Minnesota : Bearport Publishing Company, [2024] |
    Series: Healthy habits | Includes bibliographical references and index.
Identifiers: LCCN 2023028246 (print) | LCCN 2023028247 (ebook) | ISBN
    9798889162407 (library binding) | ISBN 9798889162476 (paperback) | ISBN
    9798889162537 (ebook)
Subjects: LCSH: Baths--Juvenile literature. | Hygiene--Juvenile literature.
Classification: LCC RA780 .B46 2024 (print) | LCC RA780 (ebook) | DDC
    613/.41--dc23/eng/20230710
LC record available at https://lccn.loc.gov/2023028246
LC ebook record available at https://lccn.loc.gov/2023028247

Copyright © 2024 Bearport Publishing Company. All rights reserved. No part of this publication may be reproduced in whole or in part, stored in any retrieval system, or transmitted in any form or by any means, electronic, mechanical, photocopying, recording, or otherwise, without written permission from the publisher.
For more information, write to Bearport Publishing, 5357 Penn Avenue South, Minneapolis, MN 55419.

Contents

Splash! 4

Make It a Habit 22

Glossary 23

Index 24

Read More 24

Learn More Online. 24

About the Author 24

Splash!

I turn on the water.

Then, I rub some **soap** on my hands.

Let's make some bubbles!

Pop!

5

Keeping clean is healthy.

So, I wash up every day.

This makes it a **habit**.

7

Sometimes, I get dirty during the day.

Washing gets me clean again.

Soap and water help get rid of dirt.

9

Small **germs** are on my hands, too.

I cannot see them.

But they can make me sick!

Washing with soap and water kills germs.

11

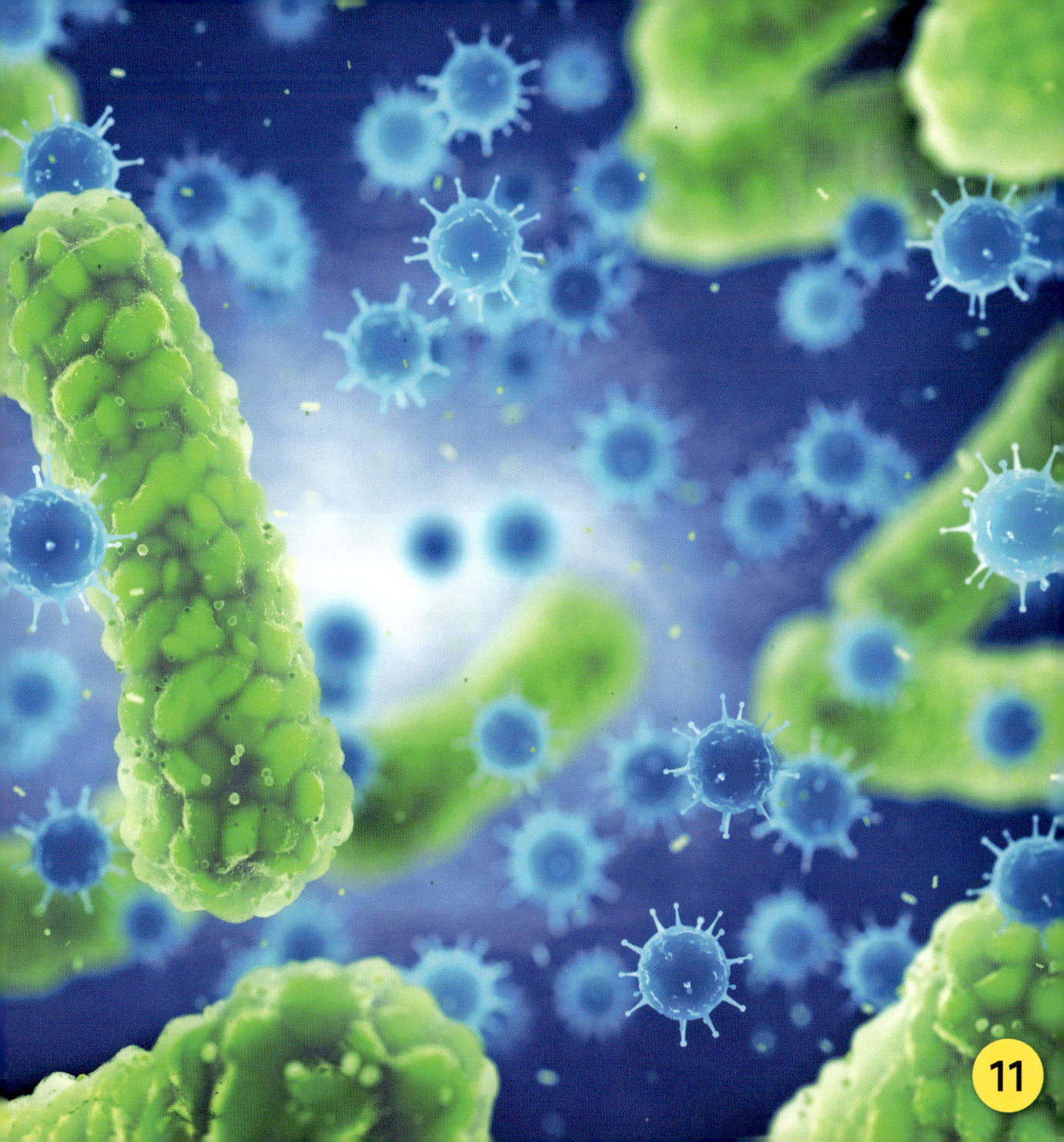

I wash my face to start the day.

This helps me wake up.

At night, I wash my face, again.

It cleans off the dirt from the day.

13

After playing outside, I take a bath.

I put **shampoo** in my hair.

Soap cleans my body.

An adult helps me stay safe in the tub.

15

Sometimes, I do not need a bath.

But I still want to clean up.

I get a washcloth wet.

Then, I wipe my body.

17

I wash my hands after I use the **bathroom**, too.

I also do it before every meal.

Then, I dry my hands on a clean towel.

19

I wash up every day.

That makes it a habit.

Washing up keeps me healthy.

I love feeling clean!

21

Make It a Habit

A habit is something you do every day. What are ways we can make washing up a habit?

Sing "Happy Birthday" to yourself to make sure you wash your hands long enough.

Put your soap and shampoo together so they are easy to grab at bath time.

Keep a small bottle of hand **sanitizer** in your pocket. Use it to clean your hands if you do not have a sink and soap.

Glossary

bathroom a place for washing and using the toilet

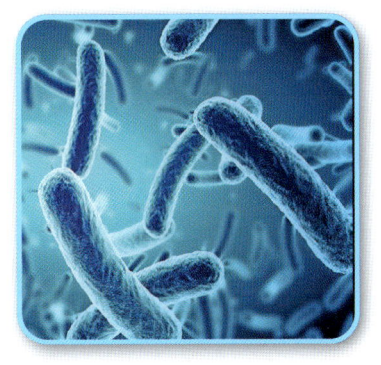

germs tiny living things that can make you sick

habit something done regularly

sanitizer something that kills germs

shampoo special cleaner for hair

soap a cleaner for skin

Index

bath 14, 16, 22
bathroom 18
germs 10
healthy 6, 20
shampoo 14, 22
soap 4, 8, 10, 14, 22
towel 18

Read More

Carr, Matt. *Now Wash Your Hands!* New York: Scholastic Press, 2020.

Schuette, Sarah L. *Health Safety (Little Pebble. Staying Safe!).* North Mankato, MN: Pebble, 2020.

Learn More Online

1. Go to **www.factsurfer.com** or scan the QR code below.
2. Enter **"Healthy Habits Washing"** into the search box.
3. Click on the cover of this book to see a list of websites.

About the Author

Emma Carlson Berne lives with her family in Cincinnati, Ohio. She loves hot baths!